D1303219

The Historic Fight for the 2008 Democratic Presidential Nomination
THE OBAMA VIEW

Senator Barack Obama held one of his many town meetings in Metropolis, Illinois, home of the DC Comics superhero Superman.

Mitchell Lane
PUBLISHERS
P.O. Box 196
Hockessin, Delaware 19707

Obama's 2008 Election Platform on . . .

Economy	Provide a tax cut for working families; provide tax relief for small businesses and startups; fight for fair trade
Foreign Policy	Secure loose nuclear materials from terrorists; pursue tough, direct diplomacy without preconditions to end the threat from Iran; renew American diplomacy
Health Care	Make health insurance affordable and accessible to all; lower health care costs; promote public health
Homeland Security	Defeat terrorism worldwide; prevent nuclear terrorism; strengthen American biosecurity

Clinton's 2008 Election Platform on . . .

Economy	Protect the next generation by paying off the United States' debt; reduce outsourcing—bring more jobs back home; reduce taxes within a balanced budget
Foreign Policy	Fight terrorism with cooperation; become more engaged in world affairs involving human rights; lead by staying engaged with the rest of the world
Health Care	Support universal health care; increase the commitment to the Global AIDS crisis; implement high penalties for underage smoking; strengthen the Medicare program
Homeland Security	Support a nuclear test ban treaty; reauthorize the Patriot Act (excluding the wiretap provision)

2008 UNITED STATES DEMOCRATIC PARTY PRESIDENTIAL CANDIDATES

The Historic Fight for the
2008 Democratic Presidential Nomination

THE OBAMA VIEW

In a dramatic and suspenseful election year, Barack Obama came from behind to win both the Democratic nomination and the presidential election.

Karen Bush Gibson

Copyright © 2009 by Mitchell Lane Publishers, Inc. All rights reserved. No part of this book may be reproduced without written permission from the publisher. Printed and bound in the United States of America.

Printing   1   2   3   4   5   6   7   8   9

Library of Congress Cataloging-in-Publication Data
Gibson, Karen Bush.
 The historic fight for the 2008 democratic presidential nomination : the Obama view / by Karen Bush Gibson.
     p. cm. — (Monumental milestones)
 Includes bibliographical references and index.
 ISBN 978-1-58415-732-8 (library bound)
 1. Obama, Barack—Juvenile literature. 2. Presidential candidates—United States—Biography—Juvenile literature. 3. Presidents—United States—Election—2008—Juvenile literature. 4. African American legislators—Biography—Juvenile literature. 5. Legislators—United States—Biography—Juvenile literature. 6. United States. Congress. Senate—Biography—Juvenile literature. I. Title.
 E901.1.O23G53 2009
 973.931092—dc22
 [B]

                                                          2008053464

ABOUT THE AUTHOR: Karen Bush Gibson writes frequently about people, places, and events for the school library market. Recent books from Mitchell Lane Publishers include *The Vietnam War* and *Langston Hughes*. Although she's lost count of how many elections she's voted in, she can honestly say that the election of Barack Obama was the most interesting and exciting election she has ever known. She lives in Oklahoma.

PUBLISHER'S NOTE: This story is based on the author's extensive research, which she believes to be accurate. Documentation of such research is contained on page 46.

    The internet sites referenced herein were active as of the publication date. Due to the fleeting nature of some web sites, we cannot guarantee they will all be active when you are reading this book.

The Historic Fight for the
2008 Democratic Presidential Nomination

THE OBAMA VIEW

Contents

*For Your Information

As an Illinois state senator running for the U.S. Senate, Barack Obama was chosen to give the keynote speech at the 2004 Democratic National Convention in Boston.

That speech, which endorsed John Kerry for the Democratic presidential nomination, thrust Obama into the national political limelight. It also may have helped him clinch the Senate seat that year.

"The Audacity of Hope"

In the summer of 2000, after a string of successes as an Illinois state senator, Barack Obama decided to take it to the next level—the United States Congress. He ran against four-term incumbent Bobby Rush.

Political analysts had taken notice of the young state senator with the odd name. After all, he had easily won two terms to the Illinois senate, representing the Chicago district where he had once worked tirelessly as a community organizer. Working for change at the federal level seemed like a logical next step, but when it came time for the votes to be counted, Barack Obama lost the race—soundly.

Some say he lost because he missed an important vote on gun control. The Obama family had been in Hawaii visiting Barack's grandmother for the 1999 Christmas holidays when a special session was called in the Illinois senate. Unfortunately, his eighteen-month-old daughter, Malia, became sick—too sick to fly on an airplane. Obama missed a very close vote, and the measure failed. Although his absence was practically unavoidable, it was a political misstep, and one that Obama's opponent publicized widely.

"It was an ill-considered race, and I lost badly—the sort of drubbing that awakens you to the fact that life is not obliged to work out as you planned,"[1] Obama wrote in his book *The Audacity of Hope*.

After the election loss, Obama worked even harder in the Illinois senate. The Harvard-educated lawyer had a knack for understanding various issues, from education to the death penalty.

Another of Obama's talents was working with the Republican legislators who dominated Illinois state government. By 2000, Democrats and Republicans were strongly partisan—meaning they didn't always work well together. They were much more likely to disagree and argue with the opposite political party than to work together to solve a problem.

Obama, a Democrat, didn't see Republicans as the enemy. During his community organizing days, Obama would tell the people he worked with that the opposing sides were just trying to do the best job for the people who elected them. According to Loretta Augustine-Herron, who was on the board that hired Obama for the community organizing job, Obama said, "You've got to bring people together. If you exclude people, you're only weakening yourself."[2]

With his Republican colleagues, Obama worked on legislation for early childhood education, tax cuts for lower income families, and a significant campaign reform bill for Illinois that's been called one of the best in the country.

On December 8, 2003, Obama filed a petition, signed by hundreds of supporters, to list him as a candidate for the U.S. Senate seat for Illinois.

Perhaps one of his greatest successes was in crime reform. While people disagree about the use of the death penalty, Obama believed that no one wanted to see an innocent person on death row. He introduced legislation requiring interrogations and confessions to be taped. With a vote of 58 to 0, Illinois became the first state to require mandatory taping.

"What impressed me about him was his ability in working with people of the opposite party. He had definite ideas about what ought to be contained in a campaign finance reform measure, but he also was willing to recognize that he was probably not going to get everything he wanted,"[3] said Mike Lawrence, director of the Southern Illinois University Public Policy Institute.

The memory of the election loss lingered. A media consultant told Obama that running for any office with the name Barack Obama would probably be unsuccessful. It was after the September 11, 2001, terrorist attacks, and newspaper headlines were focused on Al-Qaeda leader Osama bin Laden and his associates. Americans were suspicious of foreign-sounding names. But as Obama would later say in a speech, "In a tolerant America, your name is no barrier to success."[4]

Obama took a hard look at where he had been and where he wanted to go in his professional life. He recalled another Illinois politician, Abraham Lincoln, who also had setbacks, including losing an election. Obama had long admired Lincoln's insight, humility, and effectiveness. "But through his will and his words, he moved a nation and helped free a people,"[5] Obama said.

With renewed conviction, Barack Obama entered the 2004 U.S. Senate race, running against six others in the primary. Against stiff odds, he won the primary and found himself pitted against conservative Republican Alan Keyes.

Yet something interesting happened during Obama's Senate run. People outside of Illinois started paying attention too, particularly when Obama was tapped to give the keynote address at the Democratic National Convention that would officially nominate John Kerry as the Democratic presidential candidate.

On July 27, 2004, Obama ascended the podium at Fleet Center in Boston among thousands, looking not like an inexperienced state senator, but like a man with something on his mind. "Tonight is a particular honor for me because,

In the 2004 U.S. Senate race, Barack Obama (left) and Alan Keyes met for several debates across Illinois. Obama won the seat with nearly 70 percent of the vote.

let's face it, my presence on this stage is pretty unlikely."[6] He went on to tell the crowd about his father's family and the magical place called America.

For 17 minutes, Barack Obama spoke about what it meant to be an American and everything that Americans share regardless of their heritage. He spoke of economics, education, and energy issues that the government needed to address. He spoke of the terrible toll the war in Iraq was costing America. He spoke with confidence, addressing his audience on a personal level: ". . . there is not a liberal America and a conservative America—there is the United States of America. There is not a black America and white America and Latino America and Asian America; there's the United States of America."[7] The crowd cheered and chanted, "Obama." They waved "Obama '04" signs, supporting his election to the Senate.

The seed was planted. Obama won the U.S. Senate race to become the fifth African American senator, and the third elected by popular vote. It was just the beginning. With his intelligence and commitment—and his "audacity of hope"[8]—people recognized Barack Obama's potential to be the next president of the United States.

Barack Obama has been compared to many great men, from Franklin D. Roosevelt to John F. Kennedy to Martin Luther King Jr. But the politician whom Obama may most admire is a Republican—Abraham Lincoln. Born in Kentucky on February 12, 1809, Lincoln grew up in Indiana and Illinois. As a young man, he worked in a store, farmed, and split rails for fences. In his spare time, he read and learned until he became a lawyer.

After serving eight years as a state legislator in Illinois, he ran for the U.S. Senate, debating his opponent, Stephen A. Douglas, in towns across America. He lost that race, but people liked what he'd said in the debates so much that he was elected president two years later, in 1860.

With the threat of civil war looming, Lincoln reassured everyone in his inaugural address that he would do all he could to "preserve, protect, and defend" the government. Despite his words and his efforts, the southern states seceded and formed the Confederacy, and the Civil War began.

Abraham Lincoln (left) and Stephen A. Douglas on the campaign trail

Lincoln took his responsibilities as president very seriously. He issued the Emancipation Proclamation, freeing the slaves, on the first day of 1863. Like Obama, Lincoln was an eloquent speaker. His words in dedicating a military cemetery—the Gettysburg Address—have been memorized for generations. After he was reelected in 1864, the war ended, and Lincoln was looking forward to governing a peaceful nation. He urged forgiveness of Southerners and moving ahead. Lincoln's own future was limited, however. On April 14, 1865, he was assassinated by John Wilkes Booth. Lincoln, nicknamed "The Great Emancipator," is one of the most popular and well-known presidents of all time. The Lincoln Memorial in Washington, D.C., was erected to honor the sixteenth president of the United States.

Statue of Abraham Lincoln at Union Square Park in New York City

When he ran for the Illinois senate in 2004, Obama spoke of creating jobs and improving the state's economy.

Improving the U.S. economy would be an important issue during the presidential race in 2008.

CHAPTER 2

"A Skinny Kid With a Funny Name"

In his 2004 keynote speech at the Democratic National Convention, Barack Obama referred to himself as a youngster as "a skinny kid with a funny name." With comments like that, it's no wonder so many people were interested in Obama's childhood. Born in Honolulu, Hawaii, on August 4, 1961, Barack Hussein Obama Jr. was named after his father, a man from a small African village in Kenya. In the Swahili language of Africa, *Barack* means "blessed."

His paternal grandfather worked as a servant to British people who lived in Kenya. Barack Obama Sr. helped his father and herded goats when he wasn't going to school. But Obama's father was smart and ambitious. He won a scholarship to study at the University of Hawaii. While there, he met a quiet female student named Ann Dunham, who happened to be white.

Ann Dunham came from Kansas, where her father, Stanley Dunham, had worked on oil rigs before enlisting for World War II. During the war, Ann's mother, Madelyn Dunham, worked on a bomber assembly line. Once the war ended, Ann's father went to college on the GI Bill. Stanley and Madelyn eventually moved to Hawaii. Ann joined them and entered college.

Barack Obama Sr. and Ann Dunham married at a time when interracial marriage was illegal in many states in the U.S. However, with its multicultural heritage, Hawaii was more tolerant in racial matters. Soon after Barack Jr. was born, his father left to continue his education at Harvard. Distance is often hard on relationships, and his parents divorced when he was two. Barack Sr. eventually returned to Kenya, where he married again. Described as an intelligent man with a booming voice, Barack Sr. wanted to do things that would benefit his country. He was often frustrated at how hard it was to bring his dreams to reality.

In Hawaii, Ann met a college student from Indonesia, Lelo Soetoro, and she married him in 1967. Six-year-old Barack, now called Barry, moved to Jakarta, a city in Indonesia, with his mother and stepfather. A few years later his sister, Maya, was born. At age ten, Barry returned to Hawaii to live with his grandparents in their apartment and to attend Punahou School.

In fifth grade, Barry received the first and only visit from his father. He didn't know what to make of his father, who stayed for a month. One particular incident that stuck out was his father refusing to let him watch the annual showing of *How the Grinch Stole Christmas*, insisting that Barry study instead. After giving his son a basketball and a recording of African music, Barack Sr. returned to Africa. Barry never saw his father again.

Another divorce had brought Barry's mother and sister back to Hawaii. As a single mother, life was sometimes difficult. Obama remembered having to live on food stamps at one point. His mother returned to college, majoring in anthropology. She also taught her children the importance of public service.

Obama sometimes speaks of how hard both his mother and grandmother worked. His grandmother, whom he called Toot (short for *Tutu*, or "grandparent" in Hawaiian), started as a secretary at a bank and worked her way up to be one of the first bank vice-presidents in Hawaii. "But I also saw how she ultimately hit a glass ceiling—how men no more qualified than she was kept moving up the corporate ladder ahead of her,"[1] he said.

Barry left Hawaii to attend a small liberal arts college in California called Occidental College. Sometimes, college students pay more attention to parties than to their classes, and according to Obama, he spent enough time doing things outside of class that his mother called him a "good time Charlie." However, Barry Obama also spent some constructive time at Occidental. He talked with fellow students about world events, such as apartheid in South Africa and the Soviet invasion of Afghanistan.

Concerned about events in the U.S. and the world, a more serious Obama changed his name from Barry to Barack. He also transferred to Columbia University in New York. There, Obama received a phone call to tell him that his father had died in an auto accident.

After earning a political science degree in 1983, Obama briefly worked as a financial consultant, but he wasn't happy. Remembering what his mother had taught him about helping others, he thought that he might be better suited to a life in public service. One day while looking at the help wanted ads in the newspaper, Obama saw an ad for a community organizer for the Developing Communities Project in Chicago. Gerald Kellman, the activist who had placed the ad, interviewed Obama and found an intelligent, well-spoken young man. "He said he wanted to make fundamental change, he wanted to make it from the grass roots and he wanted to learn,"[2] Kellman recalled. Obama was hired for about $13,000 a year.

"Baby Face Obama," as some of the people in the community referred to him, was a hard worker. He wasn't afraid to let people know that he had no experience, but he impressed them by doing exactly what a community organizer was supposed to do—empower the people he worked with. With his help, the people of the Altgeld Gardens public housing project defined their problems and worked together for school reform, job training centers, and hazardous waste removal from homes.

As much as Obama did for the residents of Altgeld Gardens in the mid-1980s, they did even more for him. They gave him the sense of community that had been lacking in his life as he moved from place to place while growing up. Meanwhile, Obama joined Trinity United Church of Christ. Working as a community organizer also gave him some direction for his life. According to his wife, Michelle, the job "helped him decide how he would impact the world."[3]

As fulfilling as community organizing was, Obama was also frustrated by the limitations for change at the local level. After a couple of years at the job, he attended a conference at Harvard University that reawakened his desire to be a lawyer. His father had been dead for five years, but Obama thought of his father's time at Harvard and how his life hadn't turned out the way he wanted. While his father had essentially been a stranger to him, he was often on Obama's mind. Before he started down his next path at Harvard Law School, Obama needed to confront his past. He left for Kenya, where he met his father's mother, several half siblings, and assorted other relatives. At his father's tombstone, Obama started to make peace with his father. He would later complete the process when he wrote his 1995 memoir, *Dreams from My Father: A Story of Race and Inheritance*.

When Obama returned, he paid $500 for a used yellow car that looked like "an overripe banana"[4] with a hole in the floorboard. The car got him to

Boston, where he entered Harvard Law School and became the first African-American president of the prestigious *Harvard Law Review*. Summers were spent as a legal intern at different law firms. During one summer while interning at Chicago's Sidley and Austin firm, he met a corporate lawyer named Michelle Robinson.

Unlike Obama's haphazard childhood, hers had been stable. She was born and raised in Chicago. Living on the top floor of a bungalow with her parents, Fraser and Marian Robinson, and her older brother, Craig, Michelle attended Chicago public schools. Her father worked at a water filtration plant, even after he was diagnosed with multiple sclerosis at age thirty. Her mother stayed home and raised the children. Michelle graduated from Princeton University before attending Harvard Law School. She was also bitten by the public service bug and eventually left corporate law to work for the city of Chicago. She successfully headed an AmeriCorps program called Public Allies that trained young people for public service. She also founded a community center that connected the University of Chicago to the neighborhoods surrounding it.

After graduating in 1991, Obama returned to the city he thought of as home, Chicago. He worked as a civil rights attorney and taught constitutional law at the University of Chicago Law School. He and Michelle Robinson married in 1992.

The Obamas had a very full life. While Barack taught and practiced law, Michelle worked as the associate dean of student services and later community affairs for the University of Chicago Medical School. Two daughters were born: Malia in 1998 and Sasha in 2001.

A few years after Barack married, his mother died of ovarian cancer. According to Obama, his mother was "the kindest, most generous spirit I have ever known."[5] Now both of his parents were gone.

Obama recognized that it was his father's absence rather than his presence that had so deeply affected him. Because of this, family and fatherhood were very important to Barack. After assuring himself that he could make time for family, he ran for office. Campaigning would often take him on the road, but he called home every chance he got.

Although Barack Obama never lived in Kenya, it is a very important part of his heritage. His father was born in the East African nation, and his paternal grandmother and half siblings also lived there. He has a close relationship with sister Auma and his brother Abongo, who served as best man at Barack and Michelle's wedding.

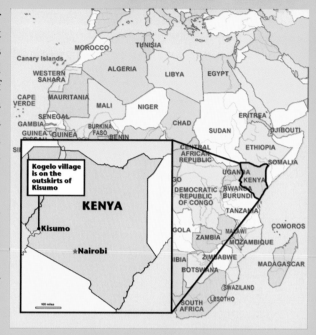

About twice the size of the state of Nevada, Kenya became an independent nation in 1963; Kenyans celebrate their independence day on December 12. The coastal areas are tropical while the interior is desertlike. Glaciers shroud Mount Kenya, which is the second highest point in Africa. Both droughts and flooding trouble Kenya, yet a fertile plateau in the western part of the country is one of the most successful agricultural areas in Africa.

Kenya boasts a population of almost 38 million people, but is troubled with high death rates from infant mortality and AIDS. It also takes in a large number of refugees from Uganda, Somalia, Sudan, and Ethiopia. While several indigenous languages are spoken in Kenya, the primary languages are Swahili and English. Unfortunately, Kenya saw some violence and fraud surrounding elections in the 1990s, and again in 2007, when 1,500 people died in election-related violence.

The people of Kenya were proud that the son of one of their own was running for president of the United States. After election day, Kenyan President Mwai Kibaki made November 6 a public holiday in honor of Barack Obama. In Kogelo, the village in western Kenya where Obama's family is from, residents cheered and danced to the news of Barack Obama's win.

Kenyan President Mwai Kibaki

Sasha, Barack, Malia, and Michelle Obama (left to right) stand on the steps of the Old State Capitol in Springfield, Illinois, on February 10, 2008.

Barack Obama had just announced his intention to run for the Democratic nomination for president of the United States.

A Grassroots Campaign

On February 10, 2007, Barack Obama stood in front of a crowd of 17,000 in the town square of Springfield, Illinois. Amid shouts of "Obama, Obama," a palpable excitement could be felt. Obama mentioned the former U.S. president for whom he felt such an affinity—Abraham Lincoln—and then said: "And that is why, in the shadow of the Old State Capitol, where Lincoln once called on a divided house to stand together, where common hopes and common dreams still live, I stand before you today to announce my candidacy for president of the United States of America."[1]

Although thousands were present to hear Obama's much anticipated announcement, millions of Americans had never heard of him—but that would soon change. After campaigning for other Democrats across the United States, Obama believed that Americans were ready for a new kind of politics, politics that united people instead of dividing them.

The first things that the American public noticed about Barack Obama was that he was an African American with a very non-American-sounding name. Obama explained where his name came from to anyone who wanted to know. And he certainly wasn't the first African American to run for president. Jesse Jackson, Al Sharpton, and Carol Moseley Braun had run for the Democratic nomination in previous years.

People also commented on Obama's apparent lack of political experience. Obama believed he had the exact experience needed from his work as a community rights organizer, civil rights attorney, and state legislator. Additionally, he had had a productive first two years as a United States Senator.

Just as Obama had worked well with Republicans in the Illinois state legislature, he continued this practice on the federal level. The first bill Obama successfully passed was with Oklahoma Republican senator Tom Coburn. Their

When the primary season began, eight hopefuls were vying for the Democratic nomination. From left to right, the candidates were Senator Joseph Biden, Senator Christopher Dodd, Governor Bill Richardson, Senator Barack Obama, former Senator John Edwards, Representative Dennis Kucinich, Senator Hillary Clinton, and former Senator Mike Gravel.

bill allowed Americans to go online to see how tax dollars were being spent. Obama also stayed busy in the Senate with ethics reform and promoting the use of alternative fuels.

The Obama campaign continued building momentum. Although Obama was an eloquent, knowledgeable speaker who drew crowds, a lot of credit had to go to the exceptional team of experts that he pulled together: Robert Gibbs as his communications chief, Julianna Smoot as the national finance director, and David Axelrod as a political consultant. Former congressional aide David Plouffe was named campaign manager.

The superorganized Plouffe made use of all the modern technology at his disposal, particularly the Internet. Interested and curious voters could find information about the issues, videos of speeches, biographical information, and opportunities to join the campaign at the site barackobama.com. Most of all, Plouffe made the public a part of the campaign. On the web site, he posted this message: "From the beginning, we've urged you to think of this as your campaign; to contribute your ideas, energy and creativity to the mission of ending a war, challenging our broken politics and changing our course."[2]

The plan was to convert the online attention into action. In an event held on March 31, 2007, the Obama campaign urged Internet supporters to meet face to face in places like the Onawa, Iowa, library. It e-mailed supporters, telling them: "The movement for change begins with you. It's one thing to understand that in theory. It's another to sit in a room full of motivated people, make a plan and then witness the effects of hard work."[3]

If online supporters could become actual volunteers, they could help motivate the voters in states like Iowa and New Hampshire, where the first primaries would be held. It was also hoped that the online numbers would translate into donations to fund the campaign. The campaign encouraged people to make $5 or $10 donations. They did, but some also made sizable contributions. In the first three months of 2007, Obama received more than 100,000 donations. By April, he had raised almost as much money as Hillary Clinton.

In July 2007, the eight Democratic candidates participated in a debate sponsored by the news channel CNN and the social networking site YouTube. All eyes were on Senator Hillary Clinton of New York, who focused on her experience for the job. Yet people also tuned in to see the relatively unknown Barack Obama. Many liked what he had to say about change in government.

In late 2007, the candidates concentrated on the first caucuses of the 2008 election year. Obama staff and volunteers passed out volunteer postcards and collected e-mail addresses as Obama spoke to voters at event after event throughout Iowa—in Ames, Cedar Rapids, Iowa Falls, and Waterloo. The grassroots campaign had taken off. It became apparent that Democratic attention was focused mainly on three candidates: Hillary Clinton, John Edwards, and Barack Obama. A late 2007 poll by the *Des Moines Register* showed Clinton in the lead with 29 percent of the vote. Edwards followed with 23 percent, and Obama came in third with 22 percent.

As the Democratic candidates campaigned in Iowa, New Hampshire, and the states that would participate in the Super Tuesday primaries on February 5, Obama picked up some endorsements from organizations and notable people, including the well-known political family the Kennedys. Like former president John F. Kennedy, Obama was a charismatic speaker. According to Caroline Kennedy, daughter of President Kennedy, Obama had the ability "to unite this entire nation around a common purpose."[4]

Another prominent Obama supporter was talk show host Oprah Winfrey, and she did more than make a statement: She made appearances and hosted fund-raising events. The news spread that Oprah would appear at a rally on the Saturday before the Iowa caucuses. The Obama campaign hoped her appearance would generate interest among female Democrats. People who volunteered four hours for the Obama campaign would get a ticket to the Oprah appearance—and 1,385 people earned tickets.

The night before the January 3 Iowa caucuses, Obama aired a two-minute advertisement focusing on the need for change in the United States. "I'm reminded every day that I am not a perfect man. And I won't be a perfect President. But I can promise you this—I will always tell you where I stand and what I think. I will listen to you when we disagree. I will carry your voices to the White House and I will fight for you every day I'm there. So I ask you to caucus tomorrow, not just for me, but for your hopes; for your dreams; for the America you believe is possible."[5]

In order to get the nomination, a candidate needed 2,118 delegate votes from the caucuses and primaries held in the individual states. Iowa had held the first presidential caucus since 1972, and results there carried a lot of weight in an election year. To the surprise of many, Barack Obama won in the Midwestern state with 38 percent of the Democratic vote.

"The media's often remarkable affection for Obama reached a new peak after his Iowa victory,"[6] said Paul Street, a social policy researcher who referred to the attention as "Obamania." Obama's face decorated many magazine covers, including the cover of *Newsweek*, which announced, "Our Time for Change Has Come." And it wasn't just newspapers and newsmagazines, but other publications too. *Rolling Stone* magazine, long considered a monitor of what is worthy of attention in modern society, put Obama on the cover not once, but twice, with publisher Jann Wenner letting everyone know what a fan he was. "Like Abraham Lincoln, Barack Obama challenges America to rise up, to do what so many of us long to do: to summon 'the better angels of our nature.' "[7]

Clinton pulled ahead in the popular vote in the next contest, winning New Hampshire's primary on January 8. Other January caucuses or primaries were held in Michigan, Nevada, South Carolina, and Florida. By the end of January, Hillary Clinton was leading with 232 delegates. Second was Obama with 158, and coming in third with 62 delegates was John Edwards.

It was time for Super Tuesday, a day in which 22 states would hold Democratic primaries or caucuses. The outcome could make or break a candidate.

The Internet has been a part of the lives of many Americans for some time now, but until the 2008 Democratic primaries, no other candidate had reached so many voters using Facebook, MySpace, and Flickr as Barack Obama. As the first candidate to successfully use the Facebook social networking site, Obama had over a million Facebook "friends." On the Internet, people could check Obama's blog at MySpace, watch an Obama speech on YouTube or iTunes, and view over 53,000 Obama photos at Flickr. The many social networking and streaming sites on the Internet provided another way for Obama to connect to and stay linked to voters. According to web strategist Jeremiah Owyang, Obama dominated social media sites partly because he jumped on the Internet bandwagon early in his campaign. Both Facebook and MySpace showed Obama with 380 percent more supporters than Republican front-runner John McCain. During his two years of campaigning, users uploaded 1,792 Obama videos, with over 18 million viewings on YouTube.

The strong Internet presence led *The Washington Post* to call Barack Obama "the king of social networking."[8] In addition to the most popular social media sites, Obama was the first candidate to post a profile on Eons, a site similar to MySpace for older voters, and to have a LinkedIn group. He also posted profiles on social networking sites for Latinos, Asian Americans, and African Americans. The Obama campaign established its own social networking site at my.barackobama.com, which allowed users to create an account, then use the site to connect with other supporters, find local events, and even blog their own stories.

Much of the success of Barack Obama's Internet presence is due to campaign manager David Plouffe, who was also in charge of Obama's 2004 run for the Senate. Plouffe encouraged the Internet community to participate in the campaign. He urged: "At the end of the day, each of you will decide how best to express yourselves in the town square of the Internet, which is helping to rekindle America's civic life."[9]

David Plouffe, who was raised in Wilmington, Delaware, and graduated from St. Mark's High School there, has been a campaign manager for Senate and presidential hopefuls since he left the University of Delaware in 1988. He managed 5,000 paid employees and thousands of volunteers during Obama's 2008 presidential campaign.

"Change we can believe in" was a frequent message of Obama's presidential campaign. The message was meant to attract the notice of voters who were unhappy with the policies and decisions of the Bush administration.

Campaigning for president requires a lot of traveling and even more speeches. Obama gave speeches, participated in debates, and visited dozens of states before their primaries.

CHANGE
WE CAN BELIEVE IN

The Momentum Builds

When the results of the first primaries and caucuses were in, candidates started dropping out of the race. John Edwards withdrew on January 30, 2008, leaving only two contenders: Hillary Clinton and Barack Obama. Although Clinton and Obama actually agreed with each other on most issues, arguments and sharp words had already been traded on the campaign trail.

The two candidates held another debate, this time in California, on January 31. It was the last debate before Super Tuesday, in which 1,681 delegates were at stake. California, a state with 441 delegates, would vote on Super Tuesday.

The debate was much friendlier than previous ones, with more smiles than sniping. One of the many issues on the table was the war in Iraq. Although both candidates agreed that troops needed to be withdrawn, Obama stated that he was the better candidate because he had never supported the war, unlike Clinton, who had voted for it while in the Senate.

Clinton responded, "You know, I've said many times, if I had known then what I know now, I never would have given President Bush the authority. It was a sincere vote based on my assessment at the time and what I believed he would do with the authority he was given,"[1] and then she said it was time to move forward.

When votes were counted at the end of Super Tuesday, the race was still too close to call. Clinton had 818 delegates to Obama's 730. The decision would have to wait for upcoming primaries. Texas and Ohio, with almost 400 delegates between them, would hold their primaries in March.

Throughout the campaign for the Democratic nomination, Barack Obama often gave credit to his wife, Michelle, whom he called smarter and a better speaker than he. To run for president was a decision they had reached together.

Ultimately, the decision would benefit their daughters, Malia and Sasha, because Obama planned to make the country a better place for future generations—to "bring people together to find common-sense, practical solutions to economic, health care, education, energy and security problems."[2]

Michelle Obama proved to a be a good speaker, although not everyone appreciated her style. While many people enjoyed earlier funny stories about her husband's difficulties with housekeeping chores, others were critical of them. She was criticized again when she said she had "never been more proud" of her country in choosing Obama for the Democratic nominee. It wasn't meant to be an unpatriotic remark, just a statement of her pride in her husband and her country. But the Obamas were learning that anything they said would be dissected as if under a microscope.

At the Democratic National Convention, Michelle Obama would have no difficulty telling the world why her husband should be president. "He'll achieve these goals the same way he always has—by bringing us together and reminding us how much we share and how alike we really are."[3]

Obama was no slouch when it came to speaking, either. For older voters, his speeches took them back to a time of hearing speeches by John F. Kennedy and Robert Kennedy. Great speakers act as if they're talking to each individual in the room. They rarely look at notes or stutter. They speak eloquently, in a way that seems to come from the heart. That is the way Obama addressed his audience. He was also clearly well informed, and many people described him as an intellectual.

"He would perhaps be the most officially intellectual U.S. president since Woodrow Wilson,"[4] said Street, referring to the twenty-eighth president, who had been a college professor, historian, and president of Princeton University before becoming president of the United States.

As the author of two books, Obama valued the power of words, and he made no apologies for being an intellectual—defined by journalist Nicholas D. Kristof as "a person interested in ideas and comfortable with complexity."[5]

Very important primaries were taking place in Ohio and Texas on March 4. Along the way, Obama had picked up a few more states, including Wisconsin, Hawaii, and Virginia. Both candidates were strong with certain demographics. Obama appealed to black voters and white educated voters, while Clinton's appeal reached mainly women and working-class voters. While

Obama was rapidly catching up, they both needed the large number of delegates that would be up for grabs on March 4.

In a debate held in Texas days before the primary, Clinton challenged Obama's repeated message of change by calling it "change you can Xerox."[6] She reminded voters that actions speak louder than words. The candidates found other things to disagree about, particularly health care plans and the conditions under which they would meet with Cuba's new leader, Raul Castro, brother of the previous dictator, Fidel Castro. While Clinton stated she would meet with the communist leader only if there was evidence of change in how the government operated, Obama said he would meet with Raul Castro, because diplomacy makes a big difference when talking to enemies of the U.S.

Clinton won in Ohio, but the numbers were fairly even in Texas. Still, Obama narrowed the delegate gap between himself and Clinton. After March 4, the tally was 1,424 Clinton to 1,520 Obama.

During the primaries, there were several debates among all the Democratic candidates—but by the end of January 2008, only Obama and Clinton were still in the race. Obama presented himself as a candidate who would bring change, while Clinton stressed her superior experience.

Although Obama wanted the presidential contest to transcend racial differences, remarks about race continued to surface. Perhaps most damaging to the Obama campaign was the March 2008 appearance of videos of his former pastor from Trinity United Church of Christ. The Reverend Jeremiah Wright made anti-American and racist statements about white Americans. The Obama campaign denounced his derogatory comments.

"All of the statements [made by the Reverend Wright] that have been the subject of controversy are ones that I vehemently condemn. They in no way reflect my attitudes and directly contradict my profound love for this country,"[7] said Obama in a letter titled "On My Faith and My Church," posted online at *The Huffington Post* web site. By the end of April, his campaign broke completely with Wright.

When Obama spoke on the anniversary of the death of Dr. Martin Luther King Jr. (April 4, 2008), he spoke about the economic struggles of the Memphis sanitation workers that had brought King to the city where he was assassinated. According to Obama, "It was a struggle for economic justice, for the opportunity that should be available to people of all races and all walks of life. Because Dr. King understood that the struggle for economic justice and the struggle for racial justice were really one—that each was part of a larger struggle 'for freedom, for dignity, and for humanity.' "[8]

On May 6, Obama attempted to unite the Democratic Party by reminding people that the race wasn't about voters' skin color, the type of work they did, or even whether they lived in a Red State (with more Republicans) or a Blue State (with more Democrats), but about a united quest for change in government. "This primary season may not be over, but when it is, we will have to remember who we are as Democrats—that we are the party of Jefferson and Jackson; of Roosevelt and Kennedy; and that we are at our best when we lead with principle; when we lead with conviction; when we summon an entire nation around a common purpose—a higher purpose. This fall, we intend to march forward as one Democratic Party, united by a common vision for this country."[9]

When the polls closed after the last of the primaries on June 3, people turned on their television sets and logged on to the Internet to find out the results. Barack Obama was ahead with 2,201 delegates, while Hillary held 1,896. Arizona Democratic Party Chair Don Bivens said about Obama: "He is an extraordinary leader, with the ability to bring people together across party lines to solve problems. That is exactly what our country needs right now, a pragmatic change of direction."[10]

California Congressman Jerry McNerney agreed. "Senator Obama represents hope for the future. He has inspired legions of young people who will energize our nation and help bring about the kind of change necessary to turn the incredible threats we face into opportunities."[11]

On June 7, New York Senator Hillary Clinton suspended her presidential campaign, offering her support to her opponent, Barack Obama, in an effort to mend the rift within the Democratic Party. "With every voice heard and the Party strongly united, we will elect Senator Obama President of the United States and put our nation on the path to peace and prosperity once again,"[12]

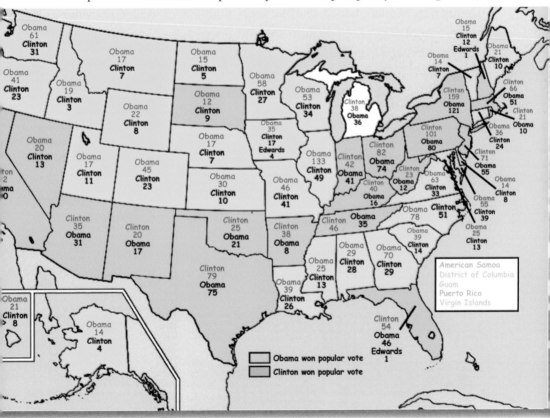

When 2008 began, the states held caucuses and primaries to vote on Democratic candidates. The winner of the popular vote in each state is shown in gold (Obama) or green (Clinton). The delegate winner of each state is in red. Obama was not on the ballot in Michigan, but the delegates there were able to vote.

she said. Then she asked her supporters to support Barack Obama as their candidate for president.

Obama's campaign staff posted a photo of Clinton on barackobama.com and urged people to send her messages of thanks. Obama also congratulated Clinton on a hard-fought, history-making campaign. "She shattered barriers on behalf of my daughters and women everywhere, who now know that there are no limits to their dreams."[13]

Clinton's name remained in the contest at the Democratic National Convention, a symbolic and historic move that was intended to unite the divided Democratic party. In particular, Obama wanted people to know that he attributed his success to hardworking women like his mother, grandmother, and wife. Democratic leaders hoped that the large numbers of women and blue-collar voters who had supported Clinton would throw their support behind Obama. They would need to if Obama was to win against the Republican nominee, John McCain, in November.

When Clinton conceded on June 7, she threw her support behind Obama.

Clinton and Obama wave to the crowds at their first joint campaign appearance in Unity, New Hampshire.

With one more hurdle cleared, Barack Obama headed into the convention in Denver, Colorado, as the Democratic nominee. The next order of business was to choose a running mate—a vice-presidential candidate. Many people wondered if he would choose Hillary Clinton. While his eventual choice wasn't Clinton, it was one of his earlier opponents in the Democratic race—Senator Joseph Biden of Delaware.

Biden filled the gaps, particularly with those voters who found Obama's experience lacking. Serving as a U.S. senator for 35 years, Biden certainly had the experience, particularly in foreign policy: He had served on the Senate Committee on Foreign Relations for many years. He had also served on the Judiciary Committee. Most people knew Biden as one of the more outspoken senators. With working-class roots in Scranton, Pennsylvania, and a Catholic background that included attending parochial schools, the campaign believed he would appeal to the working-class voters and Catholic voters that Obama needed to win the election.

Speaking at the Democratic National Convention, Obama reminded Democrats that whether they voted for him or for Clinton, they shared similar values and should work together to win the presidential race.

Obama accepts the Democratic nomination for president of the United States.

Many voters felt his choice of Biden for vice president was a strong indication that Obama could make difficult decisions well.

When Obama chose Senator Joe Biden of Delaware as his running mate, he chose an experienced senator with a reputation for speaking his mind.

On September 15, Senator Biden spoke to a Michigan audience about the need for change: "Yes, this campaign is about change, but it's about even more than that. It's about what we value as a people. . . . We know we need change if we're to restore dignity, pride, and respect."[14]

Spirits were high at Denver's convention. Just as he had four years earlier, Obama captured audience attention and turned that attention into excitement when he spoke about the election, just a little over two months away.

"I get it. I realize that I am not the likeliest candidate for this office. I don't fit the typical pedigree, and I haven't spent my career in the halls of Washington,"[15] he said. But for the thousands of people who watched the convention, Barack Obama was the best candidate. This historic presidential race was a defining moment that would allow much-needed change to come to American government.

When Barack Obama became the first African American to head *Harvard Law Review,* newspapers and publishers all wanted to know his story. So in 1995, Obama published a memoir called *Dreams from My Father: A Story of Race and Inheritance.* Slightly over ten years later, he followed it with *The Audacity of Hope: Thoughts on Reclaiming the American Dream,* a book about American politics.

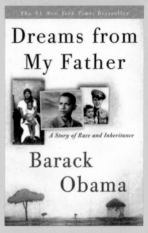

Writing was nothing new for Obama. He had written short stories when he was younger, and he had always been an enthusiastic reader. He told the American Library Association in 2005, "Reading is the gateway skill that makes all other learning possible, from complex word problems and the meaning of our history to scientific discovery and technological proficiency."[16] When reporters ask him what he's reading, he always has an answer, whether it's a biography about his hero Abraham Lincoln, or Roosevelt's first 100 days in office.

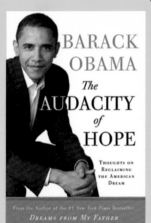

Another president who was also an author was John F. Kennedy, whose Pulitzer Prize–winning book, *Profiles in Courage,* was published four years before he was elected president in 1960. However, the book about heroic U.S. senators had long been rumored to be written in part by others, particularly Kennedy speechwriter Ted Sorensen. Other presidents have written books after leaving office, often with cowriters or ghostwriters. But no one questioned the two books Obama had written.

Dreams from My Father was reissued in 2004 as Obama was running for the U.S. Senate. The second time around, the memoir found 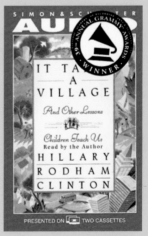 more success than the first. It also led to the first of two Grammy awards. Obama received a Grammy in 2006 for the audiobook version of *Dreams from My Father* and in 2008 for the audiobook of *The Audacity of Hope.* He wasn't the only presidential hopeful to have won a Grammy: Hillary Clinton won in the same category in 1997 for her audiobook *It Takes a Village and Other Lessons Children Teach Us.*

SEAL OF THE PRESIDENT OF THE UNITED STATES · E PLURIBUS UNIM ·

Obama and McCain shake hands at the start of the presidential debate at New York's Hofstra University on October 15, 2008.

After Barack Obama won the Democratic nomination, the presidential race was between him and Republican John McCain. The nominees met in three televised debates to discuss issues such as foreign policy and the economy.

A SECURE
RETIREMENT

A Historic Election

Barack Obama may have secured the Democratic nomination, but he still had to prove to the American people that he was the best candidate for president of the United States. One of the ways candidates get their message across is through presidential debates. Obama and the Republican candidate, John McCain, agreed to have three presidential debates at three locations.

Before the debates took place, Obama and McCain found something to agree on. The country's economy had taken a nosedive, sending the United States into one of the more serious economic crises since the Great Depression of the 1930s. Obama and McCain issued a joint statement, urging everyone to work together to support the economic bailout program that President George W. Bush had submitted to Congress.

The first debate, on September 26 at the University of Mississippi, focused on foreign policy and national security. A question-and-answer format, with questions posed by audience members, took place at the second debate on October 7 at Belmont University in Nashville, Tennessee. And finally, domestic and economic policy were discussed at the debate on October 15 at Hofstra University on Long Island, New York. In addition, the two vice presidential candidates—Joe Biden and Sarah Palin—debated on October 2, in the most-watched vice-presidential debate to date.

Obama spent a lot of time preparing and consulting with advisers before each debate. He showed a command of the facts and issues. Most of all, he was unflappable in his responses to Senator McCain. Many people suggested that Senator Obama didn't like surprises, for which journalists nicknamed him "No Drama Obama." Still, he impressed many voters as the cool, calm voice they would like to lead the country in a crisis, as opposed to McCain's hot-headed reputation.

Wanting to reiterate his points about the issues one more time before the election, Obama bought 30 minutes of airtime on the major networks. In the paid political message that aired on October 29, Obama used real people to illustrate the issues, because as he repeatedly said throughout the campaign, "everyone's got a story," whether it was a family of five who had trouble buying groceries, a retired couple with high medical bills, or a single mother struggling to keep her head above water. Obama agreed that things were bad and listed ways that he would work to get the economy back on track.

Although preliminary polls showed Obama ahead, journalists and political analysts wondered about the Bradley effect, named after Tom Bradley, an African American mayor of Los Angeles who in 1982 ran for governor of California. The polls favored Bradley to win the gubernatorial race, but when the votes were counted, his white opponent won. There have been many political races that show a significant difference between polls and voting results, leading political analysts to state that although white voters may say they'll vote for a black candidate, they don't always do so at the voting booth.

Regardless of the issues, and regardless of Obama's hard work, there was a chance that the outcome would hinge on race. After all, as much as the U.S. had progressed regarding racial equality, many people still held on to beliefs and stereotypes they had learned from earlier generations. Even students who attended racially integrated public schools felt biased against Obama because of his heritage.[1]

If people thought about race, Obama would have to hope they thought of what he had said about Dr. Martin Luther King Jr. "We have to recognize that while we each have a different past, we all share the same hopes for the future—that we'll be able to find a job that pays a decent wage, that there will be affordable health care when we get sick, that we'll be able to send our kids to college, and that after a lifetime of hard work, we'll be able to retire with security. They're common hopes, modest dreams. And they're at the heart of the struggle for freedom, dignity, and humanity that Dr. King began, and that it is our task to complete."[2]

On the night before the election, journalist Jeff Zeleny observed Senator Obama before speaking at a rally, one of many in the final days before the election. "The lines in Mr. Obama's face have grown a bit deeper since he started his campaign, with the notches of gray hair along his temples far more pronounced. He often carries the look of exhaustion."[3]

When people suggested that Obama rest, he said he would rest after the election, as he left for more speeches in swing states like Ohio and Florida that could vote either way. In addition, his grandmother, who had been such an important part of his life, was dying from cancer. Obama visited her one last time and said his good-byes, then returned to the campaign trail. She died the day before the election.

In the days leading up to the election, many locations allowed early voting at election board offices. Lines filed out the doors, down the streets, and around

As the stress of the election built for Obama, on November 3, 2008, he received the news that his grandmother passed away.

the blocks in many communities. On election day, November 4, the precincts opened and did a steady business. Barack Obama had finally returned home to Chicago to await the results with his family.

Because there are four different time zones in the continental United States, plus two more for Alaska and Hawaii, election results were scattered. The first results that came in from the eastern part of the United States showed Obama with a tremendous lead. An hour later, the polls closed in the central states. Obama was still ahead, but John McCain was gaining with the midwestern states that supported him. A close race might mean a late night for everyone. Some states were so close that they couldn't be called, yet Obama still maintained a lead, even though he still hadn't received the 270 electoral votes needed to clinch the election. Finally, polls in the Pacific time zone—California, Oregon, Washington, Hawaii—closed.

People waited in anticipation at watch parties and in front of television sets in their living rooms. Within a minute of the last of the polls closing, TV

As the polls closed on election night, the electoral votes for each candidate were tallied. The final count was Obama, 365, and McCain, 173.

Voters were jubilant in Grant Park in Chicago and in watch parties around the country when it was announced that Barack Obama would be the next president of the United States. The 2008 presidential election drew more young voters to the polls than any other race in U.S. history.

stations throughout the country flashed the same message—President-elect Barack Obama—across the screens. Different news shows aired the reactions at Democratic watch parties throughout the country. Broadcast stations kept cutting back to Chicago's Grant Park, where a quarter million people had been counting down the minutes until the West Coast polls closed. Some people had tears of joy flowing down their faces; others cheered and waved small American flags. A few days later, the tally would be final: 365 electoral votes for Obama and 173 for McCain.

Watching the returns in their Chicago home, Michelle Obama turned to her husband and said, "You are the forty-fourth president of the United States of America. Wow, what a country we live in."[4]

Barack Obama, Michelle Obama, Jill Biden, and Joe Biden greet supporters at Chicago's Grant Park after word is received that the Obama/Biden Democratic ticket won the presidential election.

When Barack Obama mounted the stage at Grant Park, the response was deafening. Several minutes of waving and smiling passed before he could begin to speak. He reminded everyone that although he had been an unlikely candidate for office, "if there is anyone out there who still doubts that America is a place where all things are possible; who still wonders if the dream of our founders is alive in our time; who still questions the power of our democracy, tonight is your answer."[5]

November 4, 2008, was the night when the son of an African man and an American woman became president of the United States. He had white grandparents who helped raise him, and he lived in Hawaii, Indonesia, California, New York, and Illinois. America has long been called a "melting pot" because of the many cultures Americans represent. With his background and history, Barack Obama embodies that American diversity.

Joseph Robinette Biden Jr. was born in Scranton, Pennsylvania, on November 20, 1942. The oldest of four children born to a car salesman and his wife, Biden was ten years old when his family moved to Claymont in New Castle County, Delaware. He graduated from the University of Delaware in 1965 with a double major in history and political science. After earning a degree from the Syracuse University College of Law in 1968, he became a trial attorney in Wilmington, Delaware.

Biden married Neilia Hunter in 1966, and three years later their first child, Joseph R. "Beau" Biden III, was born. Another son, Hunter, was born in 1970, and daughter Naomi in 1971.

Biden first served as a councilman while in his twenties before winning the U.S. Senate election at age twenty-nine, defeating longtime Republican senator Caleb "Cale" Boggs. When Biden began serving in the U.S. Senate, he was the sixth youngest U.S. senator in history—and Obama was twelve years old.

Soon after being elected the U.S. Senator from Delaware in 1972, Biden experienced a tragic loss when Neilia and Naomi died in a car accident on the way home from Christmas shopping. Biden's two sons, then two and three years old, were seriously injured in the accident. Biden almost gave up his job as U.S. Senator before it ever started. He decided to serve, taking the oath of office from his sons' hospital room. Biden's sister and brother-in-law moved in to help care for the family, and Biden made the decision to return home from Washington every night—a 90-minute train ride.

Biden continued to commute between Washington and Wilmington, even after marrying a Delaware school teacher, Jill Tracy Jacobs, in June of 1977. Together, they had a daughter, Ashley, born in 1981.

Also in 1977, Biden joined the Senate Judiciary Committee, which he would chair from 1987 to 1994. Serving as Chairman of the Senate Foreign Relations Committee, Biden is considered a foreign policy expert, but he's also been a significant voice in reducing domestic violence, drugs, and crime. After thirty-five years and five reelections, Biden was Delaware's longest-serving senator when he joined Obama on the Democratic ticket for the presidency.

Vice President Joseph Biden

Chapter Notes

Chapter 1   "The Audacity of Hope"

1. Barack Obama, *The Audacity of Hope* (New York: Crown Publishers, 2006), p. 3.

2. David Moberg, "Obama's Community Roots," *The Nation,* Volume 284, Issue 15, March 29, 2007, p. 16.

3. Peter Slevin, "Obama Forged Political Mettle in Illinois Capitol," *Washington Post,* February 9, 2007; A01. http://www. washingtonpost.com/wp-dyn/content/article/ 2007/02/08/AR2007020802262_pf.html

4. Barack Obama, "Full Text of Senator Barack Obama's Announcement for President" (Springfield, IL), February 10, 2007, http://www.barackobama. com/2007/02/10/ remarks_of_senator_barack_obam_11.php

5. CNN.com, Politics: "Obama Declares He's Running for President," May 2, 2007, http://www.cnn.com/2007/POLITICS/02/10/ obama.president/index.html

6. Barack Obama, "Keynote Address at the 2004 Democratic National Convention: 'The Audacity of Hope' " (Boston), July 27, 2004. http://www.americanrhetoric.com/ speeches/convention2004/ barackobama2004dnc.htm

7. Ibid.

8. Ibid.

Chapter 2   "A Skinny Kid With a Funny Name"

1. Barack Obama, "Remarks of Senator Barack Obama: Joint Event with Senator Hillary Clinton" (New York City), July 10, 2008. http://www.barackobama.com/2008/07/ 10/remarks_of_senator_barack_obam_92. php

2. Bob Secter and John McCormick, "Portrait of a Pragmatist," *Chicago Tribune,* March 30, 2007. http://redeye.chicagotribune. com/news/politics/chi-0703300121mar30- archive,2,6835378.story

3. Kenneth T. Walsh, "On the Streets of Chicago, a Candidate Comes of Age," *U.S. News & World Report,* Vol. 143. Issue 7, August 26, 2007, p. 34.

4. Secter and McCormick.

5. Barack Obama, *Dreams from My Father* (New York: Crown Publishers, 2004), p. xii.

Chapter 3   A Grassroots Campaign

1. Barack Obama, "Full Text of Senator Barack Obama's Announcement for President," (Springfield, IL), February 10, 2007, http://www.barackobama.com/2007/02/ 10/remarks_of_senator_barack_obam_11. php

2. David Plouffe, "A Message from David Plouffe," March 21, 2007, http://www. barackobama.com/2007/03/21/a_message_ from_david_plouffe.php

3. Chris Cillizza, "Obama Campaign Aims to Turn Online Backers into an Offline Force," *The Washington Post,* March 31, 2007, p. A03.

4. "Caroline Kennedy Endorses Barack Obama," Chicago, IL, January 26, 2008. http://www.barackobama.com/2008/01/26/ caroline_kennedy_endorses_bara.php

5. "Obama Ad Airs Across Iowa on Eve of Iowa Caucus" (Leader television ad), January 02, 2008. http://www.barackobama. com/2008/01/02/obama_ad_airs_across_ iowa_on_e.php

6. Paul Street, *Barack Obama and the Future of American Politics* (Boulder, CO: Paradigm Publishers, 2009), p. 63.

7. Jann S. Wenner, "A New Hope," *Rolling Stone,* Issue 1048, March 20, 2008, p. 35.

8. José Antonio Vargas, "Barack Obama Social Networking King," The Trail, Washington Post http://voices.washingtonpost. com/the-trail/2007/10/06/barack_obama_ social_networking.html

9. David Plouffe, "A Message from David Plouffe," March 21, 2007, http://www. barackobama.com/2007/03/21/a_message_ from_david_plouffe.php

Chapter 4   The Momentum Builds

1. "Transcript of Thursday's Democratic Presidential Debate," CNN Politics, January 31, 2008, http://www.cnn.com/2008/ POLITICS/01/31/dem.debate.transcript/

2. Judy Keen, "Obama Touts Non-political Background," *USA Today*, February 9, 2007. http://www.usatoday.com/news/washington/2007-02-09-obama-resume_x.htm

3. Michelle Obama, "Remarks of Michelle Obama and Craig Robinson—Democratic National Convention" (Denver, CO), August 25, 2008, http://www.barackobama.com/2008/08/25/remarks_of_michelle_obama_and_1.php

4. Paul Street, *Barack Obama and the Future of American Politics* (Boulder, CO: Paradigm Publishers, 2009), p. 170.

5. Nicholas D. Kristof, "Obama and the War on Brains," *The New York Times*, November 9, 2008, http://www.nytimes.com/2008/11/09/opinion/09kristof.html

6. MSNBC, "Clinton Jabs Obama Over Plagiarism Charge," February 22, 2008, http://www.msnbc.msn.com/id/23273769/

7. Barack Obama, "On My Faith and My Church," *The Huffington Post*, March 14, 2008, http://www.huffingtonpost.com/barack-obama/on-my-faith-and-my-church_b_91623.html

8. Barack Obama, "Remarks for Senator Barack Obama: Remembering Dr. Martin Luther King, Jr." (Fort Wayne, Indiana), April 4, 2008, http://www.barackobama.com/2008/04/04/remarks_for_senator_barack_oba_4.php

9. Barack Obama, "Remarks of Senator Barack Obama: Primary Night" (Raleigh, NC), May 06, 2008, http://www.barackobama.com/2008/05/06/remarks_of_senator_barack_obam_62.php

10. Don Bivens, "26.5 Superdelegates Endorse Barack Obama," Obama News and Speeches, June 3, 2008. http://www.barackobama.com/2008/06/03/265_superdelegates_endorse_bar.php

11. Ibid.

12. Hillary Clinton, "Statement from the Obama and Clinton Press Offices," Obama News and Speeches, August 14, 2008, http://www.barackobama.com/2008/08/14/statement_from_the_obama_and_c.php

13. Barack Obama, "Barack Obama on Senator Clinton's Endorsement," Obama News and Speeches, June 7, 2008, http://my.barackobama.com/page/community/post/samgrahamfelsen/gG5V2v

14. Joe Biden, "Remarks by Senator Joe Biden: The Case for Change" (Saint Clair Shores, MI), Obama News and Speeches, September 15, 2008, http://www.barackobama.com/2008/09/15/remarks_by_senator_joe_biden_t.php

15. Barack Obama, "Remarks of Senator Barack Obama: The American Promise," (Democratic Convention, Denver, CO), August 28, 2008, http://www.barackobama.com/2008/08/28/remarks_of_senator_barack_obam_108.php

16. Barack Obama, "U.S. Senator Barack Obama Addresses the American Library Association: Literacy and Education in a 21st-Century Economy," Obama News and Speeches, June 27, 2005, http://www.barackobama.com/2005/06/27/us_senator_barack_obama_addres.php

Chapter 5   A Historic Election

1. Andrea Shalal-Esa, "White Community Adapts to Obama Reality," Reuters, November 18, 2008, http://www.reuters.com/article/idUSTRE4AH8BI20081119]

2. Barack Obama, "Remarks for Senator Barack Obama: Remembering Dr. Martin Luther King, Jr." (Fort Wayne, Indiana), April 4, 2008, http://www.barackobama.com/2008/04/04/remarks_for_senator_barack_oba_4.php

3. Jeff Zeleny, "Even Keel for Obama in Final Turn to Election," *The New York Times*, November 3, 2008, p. 1.

4. *60 Minutes*, "Interview with Barack and Michelle Obama," CBS, November 16, 2008.

5. Barack Obama, "Remarks of President-Elect Barack Obama: Election Night," (Chicago), November 04, 2008, http://www.barackobama.com/2008/11/04/remarks_of_presidentelect_bara.php

6. Martin Luther King, Jr. "I Have a Dream," U.S. Constitution Online. http://www.usconstitution.net/dream.html

Obama Chronology

1961   Barack Hussein Obama Jr. is born on August 4 in Honolulu, Hawaii.

1963   Barack Hussein Obama Sr. leaves for Harvard; he and Ann Dunham, Barack "Barry" Jr.'s mother, divorce.

1967   Barry moves to Indonesia when his mother remarries.

1971   He returns to Hawaii to live with his grandparents; receives visit from his father.

1982   His father dies in a car accident.

1983   Barack Obama graduates from Columbia University in New York with a degree in political science.

1985   He moves to Chicago to work as a community organizer.

1988   He begins Harvard Law School.

1990   Obama becomes the first African American to lead *Harvard Law Review.*

1991   He graduates from Harvard Law School magna cum laude (with great distinction).

1992   He and Michelle Robinson marry.

1995   *Dreams from My Father* is published. Obama's mother dies from ovarian cancer.

1996   Obama runs for and is elected to the Illinois state legislature.

1998   Michelle and Barack's daughter Malia is born.

2000   Barack runs for a seat in the U.S. House of Representatives; he loses to Bobby Rush.

2001   Michelle and Barack's daughter Sasha is born.

2004   Barack Obama delivers the keynote address at the Democratic National Convention in Boston on July 27. *Dreams from My Father* is reprinted. Obama is elected to the U.S. Senate on November 2 with 70 percent of the vote.

2006   *Audacity of Hope: Thoughts on Reclaiming the American Dream* is published in October.

2007   Obama announces his presidential candidacy on February 10 in Springfield, Illinois.

2008   In August, Obama is declared the presidential nominee for the Democratic party. *Change We Can Believe In: Barack Obama's Plan to Renew America's Promise* is published. John McCain and Barack Obama hold debates on September 26, October 7, and October 15. Obama's beloved grandmother dies on November 3. Obama is elected the next president of the United States on November 4. On December 1, Obama asks Hillary Clinton to serve as secretary of state in his cabinet.

2009   Obama is inaugurated as the forty-fourth president of the United States on January 20.

Chronology of the Primaries

2007

January 20   Hillary Clinton announces her candidacy for the Democratic nomination.

February 10   Barack Obama formally announces that he will run for president on the Democratic ticket.

April 4   Hillary Clinton raises $26 million in the first quarter of 2007; Obama raises $25 million.

July 1   Obama raises $32.5 million in three months, far more than Clinton or any other Democratic presidential candidate.

July 23   All eight Democratic candidates debate at the Citadel in Charleston, South Carolina.

2008

January 3   Obama wins Iowa caucuses.

January 8   Clinton wins New Hampshire primary.

January 26   Obama wins South Carolina primary.

January 27	Caroline Kennedy, daughter of President John F. Kennedy, endorses Barack Obama for the nomination.
Janauary 28	Senator Edward Kennedy of Massachusetts, President Kennedy's brother, and Representative Patrick Kennedy of Rhode Island endorse Obama.
February 5	Twenty-two states hold Democratic primaries or caucuses on Super Tuesday. Obama wins 13 states, and Clinton wins 9. The delegate count is Obama 730; Clinton, 818.
March 4	Clinton wins the Ohio primary. Texas is too close to call at first, but eventually Clinton wins 65 delegates to Obama's 61.
April 22	Clinton wins the Pennsylvania primary.
May 6	Obama wins the North Carolina primary while Clinton wins Indiana. The delegate count is Obama 1,842; Clinton, 1,686.
May 14	Former Democratic presidential candidate John Edwards endorses Obama.
June 3	The last primaries take place in Montana, New Mexico, and South Dakota. Obama wins 2,201 delegates; Clinton, 1,896.
June 7	Hillary Clinton concedes and endorses Obama.
August 25–28	The Democratic National Convention is held in Denver, Colorado. Barack Obama is officially named the Democratic candidate for president.

Timeline of U.S. Elections

1776	The right to vote is awarded to white males over the age of 21 who own property and are of the Protestant religion.
1787	The Constitutional Convention of 1787 establishes the electoral college system, in which electors who represent each state determine who will be president.
1804	The electoral college system is modified when the Twelfth Amendment allows electors to cast separate votes for president and vice president.
1824	Andrew Jackson wins the popular vote but receives less than 50 percent of the electoral votes. The House of Representatives chooses John Quincy Adams as the next president.
1830	Many states drop religion and property ownership as requirements for voting; political parties emerge.
1837	Martin Van Buren becomes the first president born in America.
1870	The Fifteenth Amendment gives African American men the right to vote. However, for the next 102 years, some states will try to find ways to deny this right.
1872	Victoria Woodhull is the first woman to run for president.
1876	Although Samuel Tilden wins the popular vote, Rutherford B. Hayes receives more electoral votes and becomes president.
1888	Although Grover Cleveland wins the popular vote, Benjamin Harrison receives more electoral votes and becomes president.
1890	Wyoming becomes the first state to allow women to vote.
1913	The Seventeenth Amendment provides for the popular election of U.S. senators.
1920	Women receive the right to vote with the Nineteenth Amendment.
1940	Congress recognizes Native Americans as citizens, but it takes until 1947 for all states to grant them the right to vote.
1944	When Franklin D. Roosevelt runs for president for a fourth term, the Twenty-second Amendment is passed, limiting presidents to two terms.

1948	*Chicago Daily Tribune* prints that Thomas E. Dewey has defeated Harry S Truman. In a surprise upset, Truman wins. A famous photo is published of Truman holding the *Tribune* with the headline: "Dewey Defeats Truman."
1960	The first televised presidential debate is held between John F. Kennedy and Richard Nixon. Kennedy wins, becoming the youngest president at age 43.
1965	The Voting Rights Act is passed, which prohibits using literacy tests, poll taxes, or other restrictions to keep people from voting.
1971	The voting age is lowered to 18 years of age.
1972	Shirley Chisholm becomes the first African American to run for president.
2000	Although Al Gore wins the popular vote, George W. Bush receives more electoral votes and becomes president.
2008	Barack Obama is elected the first African American United States president.

Further Reading

For Young Adults

Brill, Marlene Targ. *Barack Obama: Working to Make a Difference* (Gateway Biographies). Minneapolis: Millbrook Press, 2006.

Davis, William Michael. *Barack Obama: The Politics of Hope* (Shapers of America). Stockton, NJ: OTTN Publishing, 2007.

Grimes, Nikki. *Barack Obama: Son of Promise, Child of Home*. New York: Simon & Schuster, 2008.

Obama, Barack. *Dreams from My Father: A Story of Race and Inheritance*. New York: Crown Publishers, 2004.

Thomas, Garen. *Yes We Can: A Biography of Barack Obama*. New York: Feiwel & Friends, 2008.

Works Consulted

Barack Obama. The Biography Channel. A & E Television Network, 2008.

Barack Obama Political Message. ABC, CBS, NBC, October 29, 2008.

Cillizza, Chris. "Obama Campaign Aims to Turn Online Backers Into an Offline Force." *The Washington Post:* March 31, 2007, p. A03.

CNN Politics: "Obama Declares He's Running for President." May 2, 2007, http://www.cnn.com/2007/POLITICS/02/10/obama.president/index.html

Keen, Judy. "Obama Touts Non-political Background." *USA Today:* February 9, 2007. http://www.usatoday.com/news/washington/2007-02-09-obama-resume_x.htm

Kristof, Nicholas D. "Obama and the War on Brains." *The New York Times:* November 9, 2008. http://www.nytimes.com/2008/11/09/opinion/09kristof.html

Moberg, David. "Obama's Community Roots." *The Nation* (Volume 284, Issue 15): April 16, 2007, p. 16.

MSNBC: "Clinton Jabs Obama Over Plagiarism Charge," February 22, 2008 http://www.msnbc.msn.com/id/23273769/

Obama, Barack. *The Audacity of Hope: Thoughts on Reclaiming the American Dream*. New York: Crown Publishers, 2006.

———. *Dreams from My Father: A Story of Race and Inheritance*. New York: Crown Publishers, 2004.

———. "On My Faith and My Church." *The Huffington Post:* March 14, 2008. http://www.huffingtonpost.com/barack-obama/on-my-faith-and-my-church_b_91623.html

Ripley, Amanda. "The Family Obama." *Time* (Vol. 172 Issue 9): September 1, 2008, pp. 46–47.

Secter, Bob, and John McCormick. "Portrait of a Pragmatist." *Chicago Tribune*, March 30, 2007. http://redeye.chicagotribune.com/news/politics/chi-0703300121mar30-archive,2,6835378.story

60 Minutes. "Interview with Barack and Michelle Obama." CBS, November 16, 2008.

Slevin, Peter. "Obama Forged Political Mettle in Illinois Capitol." *Washington Post*, February 9, 2007; A01. http://www.washingtonpost.com/wp-dyn/content/article/2007/02/08/AR2007020802262_pf.html

Street, Paul. *Barack Obama and the Future of American Politics*. Boulder, CO: Paradigm Publishers, 2009.

Von Drehle, David. "The Five Faces of Barack Obama." *Time* (Vol. 172, Issue 9): September 1, 2008, pp. 29–34.

Walsh, Kenneth T. "On the Streets of Chicago, a Candidate Comes of Age." *U.S. News & World Report* (Vol. 143, Issue 7): August 26, 2007, p. 34.

The Web Strategist: Snapshot of Presidential Candidate Social Networking Stats: Nov. 3, 2008 http://www.web-strategist.com/blog/2008/11/03/snapshot-of-presidential-candidate-social-networking-stats-nov-2-2008

Wenner, Jann S. "A New Hope." *Rolling Stone* (Issue 1048): March 20, 2008, p. 35.

Zeleny, Jeff. "Even Keel for Obama in Final Turn to Election." *The New York Times*, November 3, 2008, p. 1.

On the Internet

Barack Obama Official Website
http://www.barackobama.com

CNN Politics: Election Center 2008
http://www.cnn.com/ELECTION/2008/

C-Span: Politics
http://c-span.org/politics

The Democratic Party
http://www.democrats.org/

United States Senate: Senators
http://www.senate.gov/index.htm

The White House: Presidents of the United States
http://www.whitehouse.gov/history/presidents/

Glossary

anthropology (an-throh-PAH-luh-jee)—The study of how people have lived through time.

apartheid (uh-PAR-tyd)—Policy or laws that keep people of different races apart.

campaign (kam-PAYN)—A series of actions over a period of time aimed at achieving something, such as winning a political office.

caucus (KAW-kus)—A meeting of party members for choosing a candidate or delegates.

delegate (DEH-luh-git)—Someone who represents other people in an official capacity.

economics (eh-kuh-NAH-miks)—The study of how money, goods, and services are used in a society.

electoral (ih-LEK-tuh-rul)—Pertaining to an election, particularly the process of using delegates to determine an election.

emancipation (ih-man-suh-PAY-shun)—The act of freeing a person or group, such as from slavery.

endorsement (en-DORS-ment)—The official support of a person or thing.

ethics (EH-thiks)—Moral principles.

GI Bill—Legislation passed in 1944 that grants funds for education and home and business loans to former armed services personnel.

grass roots—Something that involves common citizens.

gubernatorial (goo-buh-nuh-TOR-ee-ul)—Pertaining to the office of governor.

incumbent (in-KUM-bent)—The person who is in office.

legislation (leh-jis-LAY-shun)—Laws that are proposed or that have been enacted by a body of lawmakers.

nomination (nah-mih-NAY-shun)—The act of suggesting someone for a job or an honor.

partisan (PAR-tih-zin)—A strong supporter of a political party or cause.

precinct (PREE-sinkt)—An area or district in a town or city.

primary (PRY-mayr-ee)—An election that will choose who will run in a main election; first.

Index